ANGELS
101

ALSO BY DOREEN VIRTUE

Books/Kits/Oracle Board

All of the above are available at your local bookstore, or may be ordered by visiting:
Hay House USA: **www.hayhouse.com®**; Hay House Australia: **www.hayhouse.com.au**;
Hay House UK: **www.hayhouse.co.uk**; Hay House South Africa: **www.hayhouse.co.za**;
Hay House India: **www.hayhouse.co.in**

Doreen's Website: **www.AngelTherapy.com**

ANGELS
101

An Introduction to
Connecting, Working, and Healing
with the Angels

DOREEN VIRTUE

HAY HOUSE, INC.

Carlsbad, California · New York City
London · Sydney · Johannesburg
Vancouver · Hong Kong · New Delhi

Published and distributed in the United States by: Hay House, Inc.: www.hayhouse.com • *Published and distributed in Australia by:* Hay House Australia Pty. Ltd.: www.hayhouse.com.au • *Published and distributed in the United Kingdom by:* Hay House UK, Ltd.: www.hayhouse.co.uk • *Published and distributed in the Republic of South Africa by:* Hay House SA (Pty), Ltd.: www.hayhouse.co.za • *Distributed in Canada by:* Raincoast Books: www.raincoast.com • *Published in India by:* Hay House Publishers India: www.hayhouse.co.in

Editorial supervision: Jill Kramer • *Design:* Charles McStravick

Library of Congress Cataloging-in-Publication Data

Virtue, Doreen.
 Angels 101 : an introduction to connecting, working, and healing with the angels / Doreen Virtue.
     p. cm.
 ISBN-13: 978-1-4019-0759-4 (hardcover)
 ISBN-10: 1-4019-0759-8 (hardcover)
 1. Angels--Miscellanea. I. Title: Angels one hundred one. II. Title: Angels one hundred and one. III. Title.
 BF1623.A53V56 2006
 202'.15--dc22

                                    2005024856

ISBN 13: 978-1-4019-4603-6
ISBN 10: 1-4019-0759-8

17 16 15 14 13 12 11 10
1st printing, June 2006

SUSTAINABLE
FORESTRY
INITIATIVE

Certified Chain of Custody
Promoting Sustainable Forestry

www.sfiprogram.org
SFI-01268

SFI label applies to the text stock

CONTENTS

WHO
ARE THE
ANGELS?

*Y*ou have guardian angels with you right now. These angels are pure beings of Divine light who are entirely trustworthy and who want to help you with every area of your life. The word *angel* means "messenger of God." Angels carry messages between the Creator and the created, like Heavenly postal carriers.

Angels love everyone unconditionally. They look past the surface and see the godliness within us all. They focus only on our Divinity and potential, and not on our "faults." So angels aren't judgmental, and they only bring love into our lives. You're safe with the angels, and you can totally trust them.

It doesn't matter whether you're a believer or a skeptic, because the angels believe in *you*. They see your inner light, they know your true talents, and they understand that you have an important life mission. They want to help you with *everything*.

Surveys show that the majority of American adults (between 72 and 85 percent, depending upon the survey) believe in angels, and 32 percent say that they've encountered an angel. So you could conclude that it's normal to believe in angels.

You don't need to have special training, be saintlike, or engage in religious work to commune with the angels. They help everyone who calls upon them, no matter what. The angels' assistance is free of charge, always available, and there are no "catches" involved.

Every day my office receives dozens of letters from people who've had angel experiences, such as hearing a life-saving warning, experiencing Divine intervention, feeling an angel's presence, or seeing an angelic apparition. The letter writers come from every walk of life and various religious and spiritual backgrounds, including agnostics and skeptics. Each person reports that they know their experience was real, and that they really did connect with their angels.

Those who regularly contact their angels report great improvements in their lives. They feel happier, more peaceful and confident, and less afraid of death or the future. They know that they're not alone, because they have trustworthy guardians watching over them.

I feel the same way. In 1995, an angel saved my life during a close brush with death. Since that day, I've been teaching about angels through my books and international workshops. I feel happier and more fulfilled than ever. It's very meaningful and touching to watch people's lives heal and improve after they begin working with angels.

Prior to my life-changing angel experience, I was a practicing psychotherapist specializing in treating eating disorders and addictions. Like most therapists, my intention was to help my clients live healthier, more meaningful lives. I've discovered that the quickest and most efficient route to happiness is through connecting with the angels.

The angels' love for us is pure. They help us hear, touch, see, and understand God in our everyday lives. So whether you need help with your health, career, love life, family, or any other area, the angels can help you. There's nothing too small or big for them to handle. They joyfully work on your behalf the moment you ask.

A Note about Religion

Although many religions speak of angels, they don't belong to any particular sect. They're truly nondenominational. Angels work with any religious or spiritual path, so you don't need to change your views or beliefs to work with angels.

The traditional idea of angels comes from the monotheistic religions of Judaism, Christianity, and Islam. *Monotheism* means a belief in one God. This faith was founded by the patriarch

Abraham who shaped Judaism, which was followed by Christianity, and then the Islamic faith. All three religions have traditions of angels providing messages and protection to their leaders and followers. In monotheism, the angel is the messenger between God and humans.

Polytheistic (meaning "many gods") religions have deities who are angelic in every way except that they don't have wings. Their deities are shared by everyone, as opposed to personal ones such as guardian angels. *Pantheistic* religions believe that God is everywhere, including within nature. These spiritual paths usually work with traditional winged angels and archangels, in addition to goddesses, elementals (another name for the nature angels), and other deities.

The point is that angels are universal archetypes, extending to ancient and modern faiths. Even though some religions may use a term other than *angel,* we're all discussing the same phenomenon of benevolent and trustworthy spiritual helpers.

Many people with fundamental Christian backgrounds call upon angels in the name of

God and Jesus. Those of the Hindu faith invoke angels, along with Ganesha, Sarasvati, and other deities central to their belief system. The same is true for other religions. The angels will work with any deities or beliefs that feel comfortable to you. After all, they're here to engender peace. You never have to be afraid that the angels would ever ask you to do anything that would make you feel afraid.

In addition, you needn't worry about being "tricked" by a lower spirit, as the angels' characteristics of love and light can't be faked, since they're gifts that come directly from God. When you meet anyone in the physical or spirit world, you can instantly feel if they're trustworthy, happy, and so on. That's why you'll recognize the angels' "calling cards," which consist of pure, Divine love. In other words, you have nothing to worry about when you connect with your angels.

I've found that those who work with angels develop a closer relationship with God, as these individuals heal fears and guilt that they may have absorbed from religious teachings.

It's interesting to me how many wars have occurred in the name of God and religion throughout Earth's history. Yet, no one ever fights about angels. It's the one part of spirituality we can all agree on. . . . everyone loves angels.

Understanding the Law of Free Will

God gave you and everyone else free will, which means that you can make your own decisions and act according to your personal beliefs. God won't interfere with your free will, and neither will the angels.

Although God and the angels already know what you need, they can't intervene without your permission. For this reason, you'll need to ask your angels to give you their assistance.

The angels will help you with anything and everything. As I mentioned before, there's nothing too big or small for them to handle. You needn't worry about bothering the angels, as they're unlimited beings who can help everyone simultaneously. Please don't think that you're pulling your angels away from more pressing matters. There's nothing more important to your angels than helping you.

Angels have unlimited time, energy, and resources. It's their sacred honor to help you in whatever way brings you peace. You can ask for their help as often as you like, without any fear of wearing them out. They love it when you call upon them!

There are many ways to ask your angels for help:

- **Say It:** Speak your request aloud, either directly to the angels or to God (the results are the same since God and the angels are one).

- **Think It:** Mentally ask your angels for help. The angels hear your thoughts with unconditional love.

- **Write It:** Pour your heart out to your angels in a letter.

- **Visualize It:** Hold a mental visual image of angels surrounding yourself, your loved ones, your vehicle, or the situation in question.

- **Affirm It:** Say an affirmation of gratitude, thanking the angels for resolving the issue.

The words you use are unimportant, because the angels respond to the "prayer of your heart," which is composed of your true feelings, desires, and questions. Angels merely need you to ask because of free will. So, it's not important *how* you ask, only *that* you ask.

Please note: All of the stories in this book are true, and the actual names of the people involved have been included unless indicated by an asterisk (*), which signifies that the person has requested anonymity.

Chapter One

THE
ANGELIC
REALM

There are countless numbers of angels who want to help you, me, and everyone live in peace. Just as people hold different specialties, so do the angels. Here is a brief guide to the various types of Heavenly beings who would love to help you:

Guardian Angels

The angels stationed permanently by your side are called *guardian angels*. These are non-human celestial entities sent directly from the Creator. They're not our deceased loved ones, who—while they can definitely act like angels—are called *spirit guides*. Our departed friends and family members, like all people living or deceased, have egos. Although they may be well-meaning, their guidance isn't as pure and trustworthy as that of guardian angels, who are with us from the moment we're born until our physical death.

No matter what we do in life, our angels will never leave us. Guardian angels are protectors and guides, ensuring that we stay safe, happy, healthy, and fulfill our life mission. Yet, we must act as a team with our guardian angels to fulfill these intentions. That means asking for help from them and then receiving the help they give you.

Speaking as a lifelong clairvoyant, I've never seen anyone without at least two guardian angels stationed by their side. One is loud and bold, to ensure that you'll work on your Divine life purpose; the other is quieter, and serves to comfort and soothe you. Yet, not everyone clearly hears their angels. If everybody did, we'd have a completely peaceful world!

You can have *more* than two guardian angels, and there are benefits to being surrounded by additional ones. They act like a castle moat, protecting you from negativity. The more angels you have with you, the stronger you'll feel the sensation of their Divine love and protection. It's also easier to hear a whole choir of angels, rather than the voice of just one or two of them.

Invoke additional angels by requesting that God send them to you, by asking the angels directly, or by visualizing yourself surrounded by more of them. You can ask for as many angels as you'd like.

Some people have additional guardian angels because a relative or good friend prayed for them to be surrounded by a number of them. Those who have had near-death experiences have extra angels to help with their adjustment to life following their experiences on the Other Side.

Every time God thinks of love, a new angel is created. That means that there's an infinite number of angels available to everyone.

Archangels

Archangels are managers overseeing our guardian angels. They are one type of the nine choirs of angels (which include angels, archangels, principalities, powers, virtues, dominions, thrones, cherubim, and seraphim). Of these forms of angels, guardian angels and archangels are the most involved with helping Earth and her inhabitants.

Compared to guardian angels, archangels are very large, loud, and powerful, yet they're also extremely loving and egoless. As nonphysical celestial beings, they don't have genders. However, their specific fortes and characteristics give them distinctive male and female energies and personas.

The Bible names Archangels Michael and Gabriel. Some versions of the Bible also list Archangels Raphael and Uriel. Ancient Jewish texts expand this list to 15 archangels.

You'll notice in the list that follows that all but two of the archangels' names end in the suffix "el," which is Hebrew for "of God" or "from God." The two exceptions were Biblical prophets who lived such exemplary lives that they ascended to archangeldom following their human lives.

These archangels are sometimes called by different names, but here are their most common ones, along with their specialties, characteristics, and brief histories:

Ariel (pronounced *AHR-ee-el*), which means "lioness of God." She helps us provide for our physical needs (such as money, shelter, and supplies). Ariel also assists with environmental causes, and the care and healing of animals. Ariel works with Archangel Raphael (who also heals and helps animals), and the angelic realm called the "thrones." Historically, she's associated with King Solomon and the Gnostics, who believed that Ariel ruled the winds.

Azrael (pronounced *Oz-rye-EL*), which translates to "whom God helps." He helps bring departed souls to Heaven, heals the grief stricken, and also assists those who are consoling the bereaved. Regarded as the "angel of death" in Hebrew and Islamic tradition, Azrael is associated with Archangel Raphael and King Solomon.

Chamuel (pronounced *SHAM-you-el*), meaning "he who sees God." He eases anxiety; brings about global and personal peace; and helps find lost objects, situations, and people. He's considered to be the leader of the angelic realm known as the "powers." Chamuel is one of the ten Sephiroth archangels of the Kabbalah, which means that he governs a pathway of the Kabbalistic Tree of Life (a mystical explanation of creation).

Gabriel (pronounced *GAB-ree-el*), which means "messenger of God." This archangel helps messengers such as writers, teachers, and journalists. Gabriel also helps parents with child-rearing, conception, or adoption.

Some faiths believe that Gabriel is a male persona, while others perceive her as feminine. Gabriel delivered the annunciation to Zacharias and Mary, as recorded in the book of Luke, announcing the forthcoming births of John the Baptist and Jesus. In the Old Testament, Gabriel saved Abraham's nephew Lot from Sodom's destruction. Mohammed said that Archangel Gabriel dictated the Koran to him.

Haniel (pronounced *Hawn-ee-EL*), meaning "glory of God." She heals women during their monthly cycles and helps with clairvoyance. She's associated with the planet Venus and the moon, and is one of the ten Sephiroth archangels in the Kabbalah. Haniel is often credited with escorting the prophet Enoch to Heaven.

Jeremiel (pronounced *Jair-ah-MY-el*), which translates to "mercy of God." He deals with emotions, helping us review and take inventory of our lives so that we may forgive, and also helps us plan for positive change. Ancient Jewish texts list Jeremiel as one of the seven core archangels. Because Baruch, a prolific first-century Jewish apocryphal author, was assisted by Jeremiel, this archangel is believed to help with prophetic visions.

Jophiel (pronounced *JO-fee-el*), which means "beauty of God." She heals negative and chaotic situations; and brings beauty and organization to our thoughts, homes, offices, and other environments, as well as lifting negativity in these areas. Some traditions call her Iofiel or Sophiel. Jophiel is known as the "patron of artists," and the Torah describes her as an upholder of Divine law.

Metatron (pronounced *MET-uh-tron*). He was the prophet Enoch, who ascended after living a virtuous life of sacred service. Metatron heals learning disorders and childhood issues, and helps with the new Indigo and Crystal Children. In ancient Jewish tradition, Metatron is an extremely important archangel, and the chief of the Sephiroth Kabbalistic archangels. The Kabbalah credits Metatron with helping Moses lead the Exodus from Egypt to Israel. The Talmud says that Metatron watches over children in Heaven, in addition to the children of Earth.

Michael. His name means "he who is like God." He releases us from fear and doubt, protects us, and clears away negativity. Usually considered the most powerful of all archangels, he's described in the Bible and other Christian, Jewish, and Islamic sacred texts as performing heroic acts of protection. Michael is the patron saint of police officers because he protects and lends courage to those who invoke him. He oversees the angelic realm known as the "virtues."

Raguel (pronounced *Rag-WELL*). His name means "friend of God." He brings harmony to all relationships, and helps to heal misunderstandings. The book of Enoch describes Raguel as the overseer of all the angels, ensuring harmonious inter-actions between them. Raguel is credited with assisting the prophet Enoch's ascen-sion and transformation into Archangel Metatron.

Raphael. His name means "he who heals." He heals ailments and guides healers and would-be healers. He's one of the three presently sainted archangels (the others being Michael and Gabriel, although at one time seven archangels were canon-ized). In the book of Tobit (a canonical Bible work), Raphael describes himself as a servant before the Glory of the Lord. He is believed to be one of the three archan-gels who visited the patriarch Abraham. Because he assisted Tobias on his jour-ney, Raphael is considered a patron saint of travelers. His main role, though, is in healing and assisting healers.

Raziel (pronounced *RAH-zee-el*). His name means "secrets of God." He heals spiritual and psychic blocks, and helps us with dream interpretations and past-life memories. Ancient Jewish lore says that Raziel sits so close to the throne of God that he hears all of the universe's secrets, which he has written down in a book called *Sefer Raziel* (which means *The Book of the Angel Raziel* in English). Legend says that Raziel gave this book to Adam as he was leaving Eden, and to Noah as he was building the ark. The Kabbalah describes Raziel as the embodiment of Divine wisdom.

Sandalphon (pronounced *SAN-dul-fon*). He was the prophet Elijah, who ascended into an archangel. He serves many purposes, including helping people to heal from aggressive tendencies and delivering our prayers to the Creator. In addition, Sandalphon helps musicians, especially those involved in using music for healing purposes. Since he was one of the two humans who ascended into archangel status, Sandalphon is considered the twin brother of Metatron (who was the prophet Enoch). Ancient Hebrew lore speaks of Sandalphon's great stature and says that Moses called Sandalphon "the tall angel."

Uriel (pronounced *YUR-ee-el*). His name means "God is light." He's an angel of wisdom and philosophy who illuminates our mind with insight and new ideas. In Hebrew sacred texts, Uriel's roles are varied and vast. As the angel of light, he's often associated with the angelic realm of the illuminated "seraphim," who are closest to God in the nine choirs of angels. Uriel is believed to be the angel who warned Noah of the impending flood. Uriel is usually identified as one of the four major archangels, including Michael, Gabriel, and Raphael.

Zadkiel (pronounced _ZAD-kee-el_). His name means "righteousness of God." He heals memory problems and assists with other mental functions. Many scholars believe that Zadkiel was the angel who prevented Abraham from sacrificing his son Isaac. The Kabbalah describes Zadkiel as a co-chieftain who assists Michael in protecting and releasing us from lower energies.

The archangels are nondenominational, meaning that you needn't belong to a particular religion in order to elicit their attention and help. Since archangels are limitless nonphysical beings, they can help everyone who calls upon them simultaneously. The archangels will respond to your requests, whether they're spoken, thought, or written. You can even ask the archangels to be permanently stationed by your side, and they're very happy to do so.

What Do Angels Look Like?

I'm often asked this question. As a child, I saw angels primarily as twinkling white and colored lights. As I grew older and my sight adjusted, I saw their shape and form. Now I see angels around everyone, everywhere I go. Their beauty is breathtaking and awe-inspiring.

Angels are translucent and semi-opaque. They have no skin, so they don't have racial colorings to their body, eyes, or hair. They glow in different colors, according to their energies. Their clothing looks like opalescent chiffon coverings.

Angels have large swanlike wings, although I've never seen one flap its wings to fly. The angels taught me that the artists who originally painted them mistook their glowing aura for halos and wings, and so portrayed them in this way. Now we expect angels to look like those paintings, so angels often appear to us as winged beings.

Angels come in all shapes and sizes, just like people. The archangels, not surprisingly, are the tallest and largest of the angels. The cherubs look like small babies with wings. Guardian angels appear three to four feet tall.

Angels are on higher-frequency wavelengths than we are. It's similar to television or radio stations being on parallel yet different bandwidths—the angels live next to us on an energy level that we can feel, and that many of us can see and hear. Whether you can sense your angels' presence right now or not, you can definitely connect with them and immediately receive their assistance, as we'll explore in the next chapter.

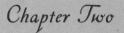

Chapter Two

CONNECTING
WITH YOUR
ANGELS

After you ask for your angels' help, they immediately go to work on your behalf. They'll do one or more of the following:

- Directly intervene and manifest your desires at exactly the right time.

- Give you a sign that they're with you.

- Give you guidance and instructions so that you'll take the appropriate steps to co-create the answer to your prayer, with their help.

Guidance and instructions are the most common ways in which angels answer our prayers. This process is called *Divine guidance.* When you receive such guidance, you must take action so that your prayer will be answered. Many people who believe that their prayers go unanswered are ignoring the information they've received.

Divine guidance is repetitive, loving, uplifting, and encouraging, and always asks us to improve a situation. It can come in one (or a combination) of four ways:

1. Physical or emotional. You get gut feelings, tingling sensations, goose bumps, an intuitive hunch, or feel the presence of an angel with you. These feelings guide you to make positive changes. This is called *clairsentience,* which means "clear feeling."

Those who receive their Divine guidance through feelings tend to be extra-sensitive to energy, other people's feelings, and chemicals. If this applies to you, you'll need to be discerning about who and what you spend time with, as you're more deeply affected than the average person.

One way to handle sensitivity is by shielding and clearing. *Shielding* means praying for spiritual protection, or visualizing protective light surrounding you. *Clearing* means asking the angels to release any negativity that you may have absorbed during the day.

After you ask your angels for answers or assistance, notice your repetitive or strong feelings. Honor these feelings and avoid any tendencies to say, "Oh, it's just my feeling." The primary way that God and the angels speak to us is through our feelings. True Divine guidance makes you feel safe and loved.

Follow any feelings that guide you to make positive changes, even if they seem illogical or unrelated to your prayer request. If you're unsure whether the feelings are true guidance, ask your angels for signs to validate them.

2. Visions and dreams. You see an image in your mind's eye, you have a very clear visitation in a dream or while awake, you see sparkling or flashing lights, or see mind movies that give you information. This is called *clairvoyance*, which means "clear seeing."

Those who receive their Divine guidance visually tend to be very sensitive to light, colors, and beauty in the physical world. If you're visually oriented, you feel best when engaged in artistic and creative expressions. You can visualize your desires being manifested, which helps you be successful in many areas.

Many people mistakenly think that clairvoyance means seeing angels with your eyes open, as three-dimensional opaque beings. While that happens occasionally, most clairvoyants see angels as fleeting ethereal images in their mind's eye. These mental images are just as valid as what you might see outside your mind's eye.

After you ask your angels for help, notice any images that come to mind, or any signs that you see with your physical eyes. If you see a vision of a "dream come true," ask your angels to guide you one step at a time toward its realization.

3. Knowingness. You know things without any rational reason, as if God has downloaded the information to you; you say or write with wisdom exceeding your present knowledge; you know how to fix an item without having to read instructions. This is called *claircognizance,* which means "clear knowing."

Those who receive their Divine guidance as "wordless words" tend to be highly intellectual and analytical. If you're thinking oriented, the answers to your prayers will come as brilliant ideas that ask you to start a business, invent something, write a book, and so forth. You're a natural channeler filled with wisdom beyond your years.

When you receive revelations and ideas, avoid the mistake of thinking that this is common knowledge or something that everyone knows. Be confident that you can awaken these Divine gifts and bring them to fruition. You can ask the angels to give you the instructions and confidence to do so.

4. Words and sounds. You hear your name called upon awakening, you hear a strain of celestial music, you overhear a conversation that seems tailor-made for you, you hear high-pitched ringing in one ear, or you hear a song in your head or on the radio that holds special meaning. This is called *clairaudience*, which means "clear hearing."

Those who receive their Divine guidance as words are very sensitive to noise and sound. If you're auditory, you'll actually hear a voice inside your head or just outside your ear. The angels always use positive and uplifting words, and it sounds as if someone else is speaking to you.

You may also hear a high-pitched ringing sound in one ear, which is the way angels download helpful information and energy. If the ringing is annoying, ask the angels to turn down the volume.

When you hear messages that ask you to take positive action, it's important to listen to them. In an emergency or time-urgent situation, the angels talk in a loud, to-the-point voice. During ordinary moments, their voices are softer, which requires you to maintain a quiet mind and environment. As you become increasingly sensitized to hearing the sweet sound of angels, you'll want to protect your ears from loud noise.

Examples of Divine Guidance

Whether they speak to us through feelings, words, visions, or thoughts, the angels' messages are always uplifting, loving, and inspirational. The angels are like air-traffic controllers who can see far ahead, behind, and to each side of us. In other words, they have more of a perspective on how our actions today will affect our future. So if the angels guide you to do something that seems unrelated to your prayers, it's because they can see how such actions benefit your future.

Here are some examples of Divine guidance topics that angels often give us:

- **Health and lifestyle:** Improving your diet; detoxing; exercising more or differently; spending time outdoors in nature

- **Spirituality:** Meditating more; doing yoga; quieting the mind, body, and home

- **Career and finances:** Following your passion; releasing money fears; reducing work stress

- **Emotions:** Letting go of worries; forgiving yourself and others; overcoming procrastination

A Reminder to Ask

There's an old adage that says "Those who write letters are the ones who receive the most mail." Well, it's the same with the angels. If you'd like to hear from your angels more often, then talk with them more often.

Share your dreams, disappointments, fears, worries, concerns, and joys with them. Tell them everything. Ask them about *everything,* as the angels want to help you with every area of your life.

Your personal relationship with your guardian angels will deepen as you speak to them regularly. One way to get to know your angels even better is to ask them their names. Just think or vocalize the request: "Angels, please tell me your names," and then notice the word that comes to you as a thought, sound, feeling, or vision. It's best to write these names down so you'll remember them (some of them may sound unusual). If you don't receive any names, it usually means that you're trying too hard to hear. Wait until you're relaxed, then ask again.

Next, say to your angels: "Please send me signs in the physical world that I'll easily notice, to help me validate that I've heard your names correctly." You'll then notice the names that you've received in people that you meet, conversations you overhear, and so forth.

Practice asking your angels questions and then listening to their replies. In time, you'll learn to instantly distinguish the voice of the angels from the voice of ego (the fearful part of us). It's similar to picking up the phone and immediately knowing whether it's a loved one or a solicitor who's calling. Also with practice, you'll learn to trust and lean upon the angels' guidance as you find success as a result of following their loving advice.

Tips for Increased Clarity

You can ask your angels to help you hear them better, or to understand the meaning of their more cryptic messages. Here are some other ways to increase the clarity of Divine communication with your angels:

— **Breathe.** When we're stressed, we often hold our breath. This blocks us from hearing the messages that could relieve our stress. So, remember to breathe deeply when you're conversing with your angels. The angels have told me that their messages are carried upon the molecules of oxygen, so the more fresh air we breathe, the louder their messages seem to be. That's why it's easier to hear your angels when you're outside in nature, or near water sources (including your shower or bathtub).

— **Relax.** Trying too hard prevents clear Divine communication. You needn't strain to hear your angels, as they're more motivated than you are to communicate. Instead, relax your body with your breath. Be in a receptive state, and ask your angels to help you release any tension in your mind or body.

— Follow their guidance. If your angels are asking you to improve your diet, it's probably because they know that processed foods and chemicals create static on the Divine communication lines. Your angels are your best teachers in guiding you on how to better hear their voice. Ask for their assistance in this regard, and then follow whatever guidance you receive.

— Ask for signs. If you're unsure whether you're accurately hearing your angels, ask them to give you a sign. It's best not to specify what type of sign you want. Allow the angels' infinite creativity to devise a wonderful sign that you'll easily recognize. You'll delight in the loving sense of humor that angels display in their use of signs, as you'll read about in the following chapter.

Chapter Three

SIGNS
FROM THE
ANGELS

The angels give us signs so that we'll know that they and their messages are real. Signs can be anything that you see or hear in the physical world three or more times, or receive in a very unusual way. For instance, if you hear the same book title from three or more different sources, then it's probably a recommendation from your angels to read that book.

The angels also leave us feathers in unusual places as a sign of their presence, probably because we associate feathers with angel wings. In the two stories that follow, the angels left feathers as a sign of reassurance of a positive outcome to stressful situations:

When Sandra's cat, Jerry, became ill, she took him to the veterinary hospital. Jerry's condition grew worse, and he went into a coma. But Sandra wasn't about to give up on her beloved cat, so she asked her angels for help. As she stepped out her front door to visit Jerry, Sandra found a white feather lying on her porch. She took this as a positive sign that the angels were helping her cat to recover.

During the following week, each time Sandra and her husband left their home to visit Jerry at the hospital, they'd find a new white feather on their porch. Sandra laid the eight feathers she'd collected on a photograph of Jerry, and continued asking God and the angels to heal her beloved cat. Finally, Jerry recovered enough to come home. His health has been wonderful for the past six years since the angels signaled Sandra through feathers that everything would turn out fine.

Like Sandra, Kathryn received so many feathers that she knew her situation would be resolved:

Kathryn had a misunderstanding with a friend, and she was considering ending the relationship, so she asked for guidance from her angels. As Kathryn sat in her backyard crying about the situation, a feather floated right past her. She took this as a sign that the angels were working on her relationship, and for her to take no action at present.

That afternoon as Kathryn walked to her children's school, she again asked her angels for a sign that her relationship would heal. She looked down and saw a feather, and then another. By the time she arrived at her destination, Kathryn had collected 35 feathers, which she took as a very positive sign. Sure enough, Kathryn and her friend resolved their misunderstanding, and they now remain very close to each other.

Another common sign is seeing angel-shaped clouds, as the following story relates:

> While riding in an ambulance on her way to have emergency heart surgery, Mary was naturally frightened. She prayed for help, and as she looked out the ambulance's back windows, Mary saw a cloud in the clear shape of an angel kneeling in prayer. Mary instantly knew that she'd be okay. She remembered the vision throughout her surgery and recovery process, with complete faith that the angels were watching over her. They were! Mary is now recovered, and very thankful for the reassuring sign that the angels sent her.

Sometimes the signs we receive come in the form of a fragrance, rather than something we see or hear. Many people report smelling perfume, flowers, or smoke when their angels are nearby:

Kathleen desperately wanted to sell her house so she could move near her daughter who was expecting her first baby in August. Frustrated one evening after buyers backed out of purchasing her home, Kathleen sat in her kitchen and cried. Suddenly her entire kitchen filled with the scent of roses. Kathleen couldn't understand this, but a friend explained to her that it was a common sign from the angels that everything would be okay. It *did* turn out fine, and Kathleen's home soon sold.

Then Kathleen needed the angels' help in finding a new place to live near her daughter. Once again, the angels came to her aid and guided her to a beautiful home at a good price. Kathleen knew that it was the right place when she saw a beautiful red rosebush in front of the home. She recalls, "There was one bright red rose standing way out among all the others, and I knew that I was home."

Angel Lights

About 50 percent of my audience members worldwide report seeing flashes of light with their physical eyes. These lights look like camera flashbulbs or shimmering sparkles. Sometimes they're white lights, and other times they're bright jewel-like shades of purple, blue, green and other colors. Several people have told me they've had their eyes examined because they worried that their visions of sparkling lights were abnormal. However, their eye doctors told them that their physical eyes were perfectly healthy.

That's because these lights have nonphysical origins. I call this phenomenon *angel lights* or *angel trails.* When you see these lights, you're seeing the friction or energy of angels moving across the room. It's a little like seeing sparks fly from a fast-moving car.

The white lights are from our guardian angels, and the colorful lights originate from archangels. Here's a list to help you know which of the archangels you're encountering when you see colored flashes or sparkles of light:

- **Beige:** Azrael, the archangel who helps us heal from grief

- **Blue** (pale, almost white): Haniel, who helps women with their feminine health, and assists with clairvoyance

- **Blue** (aqua): Raguel, who helps with relationships

- **Blue** (dark): Zadkiel, the archangel who helps us improve our memory and mental functioning

- **Green** (bright emerald): Raphael, the healing archangel

- **Green** (pale): Chamuel, the archangel of peace who helps us find whatever we're looking for

- **Green with dark pink:** Metatron, who helps children retain their spiritual gifts and self-esteem

- **Pink** (bright fuchsia): Jophiel, who helps us beautify our thoughts and life

- **Pink** (pale): Ariel, who helps with animals, nature, and manifestation

- **Purple** (bright, almost cobalt blue): Michael, who gives us courage and protection

- **Rainbows:** Raziel, who heals spiritual and psychic blocks and teaches us esoteric secrets

- **Turquoise:** Sandalphon, the musical archangel

- **Violet** (reddish purple): Jeremiel, who helps us heal our emotions

- **Yellow** (pale): Uriel, the archangel of wisdom

- **Yellow** (dark): Gabriel, who helps messengers and parents

Angel Numbers

Another common way in which the angels speak to us is by showing us number sequences. Have you ever noticed that when you look at the clock, a license plate, or a phone number that you see the same numbers repeatedly? This is not a coincidence, but rather, a message from above.

Since the era of Pythagoras (the esteemed Greek philosopher), we've known that numbers carry powerful vibrations. Musical instruments and computers are based upon mathematical formulas, and the angels' number messages are just as precise.

The basic meanings of the numbers you see are as follows:

0: This is a message of love from the Creator.

1: Watch your thoughts and only think about your desires instead of your fears, as you will attract what you're thinking about.

2: Keep the faith and don't give up hope.

3: Jesus or other ascended masters are with you and helping you.

4: The angels are assisting you with this situation.

5: A positive change is coming up for you.

6: Release any fears about the physical/material world to God and the angels. Balance your thoughts between the material and spiritual.

7: You're on the right path, so keep going!

8: Abundance is coming to you now.

9: Get to work on your life's purpose without delay.

When you see a combination of numbers, simply "add" the meanings above together. For instance, if you see 428, this would mean: "The angels are with you, so keep the faith, as abundance is coming to you now."

(See my book *Angel Numbers* for more detailed information.)

The angels speak to us in varied and creative ways, so if you feel that you're receiving an angel message, then you probably are. Ask your angels to help you recognize their signs and messages, and you'll begin to notice them all around you. The more you take note of and follow these signs with success, the more confidence you'll have in the angels and yourself.

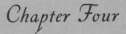

Chapter Four

ANGELIC PROTECTIONS

It's a good idea to call upon your guardian angels and also Archangel Michael for protection while driving. I also recommend visualizing your car surrounded by white light, which is the energetic essence of angels. In crowded conditions, ask the angels to protect the other cars driving near you.

The angels will protect your loved ones while they're driving even if you're not accompanying them. Simply ask the angels for whatever specific assistance you'd like, and they're happy to provide this for you.

Before you begin driving, simply ask the angels to watch over you and the other drivers, protecting everyone and ensuring a safe and pleasant journey. If you forget to do so, you can ask the angels anytime during your trip. I've even talked to people who have called upon the angels in the midst of a collision, with miraculous results.

Since the angels are above and beyond the physical world, they can intervene in mysterious ways, as Doris discovered:

Doris was driving about 50 miles per hour on a long bridge when her car's hood flew up, completely blocking her view. She felt the car swerve down the embankment and then stop inches from the deep water. Other drivers stopped to help Doris, and they all asked her if she was okay. Then they asked how her passenger was.

Doris explained that she didn't have a passenger, that she had been driving alone. The 12 people who'd witnessed the accident all said they'd seen another person in the front passenger seat. They figured that Doris was delirious from the impact and went to look for the person in the passenger seat.

Stunned, Doris thought, *Was it my guardian angel? My car just seemed to be lifted up and set back down without a dent or a scratch, and no injury came to me.*

Doris's story is fascinating in that 12 people reported seeing a person riding with her, someone who Doris concluded must have been her protective angel. I've received many stories from people who report that their cars have defied gravitational laws in inexplicable ways. After hearing so many of these stories, I believe that the only explanation is that the angels are able to move cars out of harm's way:

Estelliane was driving in the pouring rain when a semitrailer crashed into her driver's side door. She glanced at the silver angel clipped to her rearview mirror and said a prayer. Suddenly, Estelliane felt her car lift up into the air and gently land on the shoulder of the road. Remarkably, Estelliane and her passenger suffered no injuries and the car was drivable.

She says, "The car did something that is not physically possible in terms of the law of dynamics. I got hit sideways, so the car should have spun forward and hit the other cars in front of me. The little angel attached to my car mirror disappeared, but I know that my guardian angels who protected me that day are always with me."

Sometimes the angels protect us from accidents by making sure that our vehicle doesn't work. I've received many stories of car engines suddenly stopping just in time to avoid a collision:

Donna was at a three-way intersection awaiting the green light. When the light changed, she felt a force push her foot from the gas pedal. The car then stalled. At that moment, a large truck sped through the intersection, running the red light. Had Donna proceeded, she would've been sideswiped. Donna says, "I knew that the force that took my foot off the pedal was an angel. I was shaken, but grateful."

The angels can temporarily stall our cars to help us avoid accidents. In this next case, the angels disabled a car overnight while its driver sobered up:

Kathryn was upset because her boyfriend, Ben, insisted on driving, even though he'd been drinking alcohol throughout the day. As they got into the car to make a 90-mile trip, Kathryn silently prayed for protection. So she was grateful that when Ben turned the key, the car wouldn't start at all. The alternator broke at the very moment of Kathryn's prayer, ensuring that Ben wouldn't be able to drive.

I've also received many stories from people who talked about feeling an invisible pair of hands help them. The hands push them out of harm's way, hold them tightly as a car tumbles through the air, or take over turning the steering wheel:

Jacqueline lost control of her car after making a sharp U-turn. Her vehicle bounced and a rollover seemed inevitable. As she desperately tried to correct her steering, a voice said to Jacqueline, "Let go of the wheel."

Jacqueline thought, *I'll crash if I let go of the wheel,* but the voice repeated its firm but loving command. So Jacqueline relented and took her hands off the steering wheel. Ten seconds later, the car miraculously ceased skidding and stopped at the side of the road.

She says, "It was as if someone had taken over and was driving the car for me. Traffic was heavy, but during the entire time I was bouncing all over the road, no cars had passed me. It was clear that my angel had held back all of the other cars in order to keep us all safe."

Roadside Assistance

Angels not only protect us from accidents, they also help us en route. I frequently receive stories from people who were able to drive miles on empty gas tanks or flat tires, thanks to the angels. People also tell me that the angels help them get to appointments and airports on time without speeding. Angels can turn traffic signals green and find you wonderful parking places . . . just ask them!

Brenda was driving home late at night in the pouring rain. She could barely see her own headlights, much less the road. Brenda feared for her safety, but couldn't see well enough to pull off the road. Out loud, she begged the angels to give her enough light to get home safely.

Brenda explains what happened next: "I suddenly saw a brilliant light from the sky shine down." Although the rain continued to pour, the light illuminated her path and she had no problem driving. The light began to dim after 30 minutes. So Brenda again asked the angels for more light.

She says, "As if in answer, the brilliant light came back. It stayed that way until the rain finally stopped and I didn't need it anymore." The whole way home, Brenda continually repeated "Thank you" to the angels. This experience motivated Brenda to incorporate angels more fully into her life.

The angels can keep your car going even when it seems impossible, such as when your gas tank is empty, a tire is flat, or the vehicle is having mechanical problems. Of course, the angels would never ask you to drive under unsafe conditions. They'll either fix your car for you or guide you to a service station or wonderful mechanic who can help you:

Barbara was driving on an icy road when another car skidded into the front of her car. After filing the police report, she said a prayer of gratitude that she wasn't injured and asked the angels to help her car make it to a service station that she was familiar with and trusted.

Barbara recalls, "When I arrived at the service station, my car zonked out. The attendant examined the car, looked at me in awe, and said he didn't know how I'd managed to drive it anywhere. But I knew that it was the angels answering my prayers for help."

Angelic Help in the Air

My husband, Steven, and I travel worldwide giving workshops, and I depend on the angels to take care of all aspects of our arrangements, from start to finish.

For an airplane trip, you can ask your angels to:

- Help you get an extremely nice, warm, friendly, and competent customer-service representative when calling an airline to book reservations.

- Guide you on what to pack for a trip. (*Hint from personal experience:* If the angels tell you to take along an umbrella or some other item, do so even if you think it's illogical. The angels know best.)

- Arrange transportation to the airport. If you're driving yourself, they can help you find a wonderful parking space close to the terminal.

- Help you avoid lines at check-in, and work with sweet and competent airline personnel.

- Let you sail through airport security without being searched.

- Get you a wonderful seat and great seatmates (or an empty seat next to you!)

- Make certain that the airplane is mechanically safe and sound.

- Have the airplane take off and land on time.

- Ensure that you and your luggage make your connecting flights.

- Protect and deliver your baggage so that your suitcases are the first ones on the luggage carousel when you're there to collect it.

- Find you reliable transportation to your hotel.

- Help you avoid lines at hotel check-in.

- Upgrade you to a quiet and comfortable hotel room.

If you encounter turbulence on your flight, ask the angels to smooth the ride. Hundreds of them will hoist the plane and its wings on their backs, and you'll be riding on a cushion of angels. By employing these methods, Steven and I have enjoyed wonderful travel experiences for years.

Helen's* airport story is one of my favorites. It's another reminder that angels are everywhere:

It was 16-year-old Helen's first airplane trip alone, so her mother and grandmother prayed fervently for her protection.

Helen flew from Pittsburgh to Dallas, where she was to change airplanes for her final destination of Los Angeles. An older gentleman wearing plaid pants who strongly resembled Helen's grandfather approached her at the Dallas airport and asked her how she was and where she was going. Normally, Helen would have been cautious around strangers, but there was something about the man that Helen felt she could trust.

Since she was very nervous about the flight, Helen opened up to the man. Strangely enough, he seemed to already know details about her. He told Helen not to worry, that everything would be okay, and that he'd talk to her later.

Helen boarded the airplane and put the gentleman out of her mind. When she landed in Los Angeles, no one was there to meet her, so she was very frightened and confused. As Helen waited for her father, the older gentleman with the plaid pants sat next to her! This surprised her, as she hadn't seen him anywhere on her plane from Dallas to Los Angeles.

The man said, "I thought you'd still be here. I'll just wait until your father comes so you aren't alone." When her dad arrived, Helen turned to introduce her father to the man, but he'd disappeared. Helen told her father that she was talking to the man just a moment before he'd arrived. Her father replied, "I saw you talking all right, but I just thought you were talking to yourself."

A few weeks later, Helen was back home in Pittsburgh attending her church's fund-raiser. She felt a tap on her shoulder, turned around, and was astonished to see the old gentleman wearing the same bright plaid pants smiling at her. He said, "I told you everything would be all right, and now you're home safe." No one else at the church bazaar saw the man.

Helen ran home and related the whole story to her grandmother, who said, "I prayed for you to have a guardian angel, and my prayers were answered."

Helen says, "I know that it sounds unbelievable, but it's true. I've never, ever doubted angels, and now that my grandmother is in Heaven, I also feel that she's with my angels, too."

Protection in Other Ways

In addition to protecting us while we're traveling, the angels also keep us safe at home, work, and school. It's a good idea as you fall asleep to ask the angels to stay posted at your windows and doors throughout the night. You'll sleep soundly knowing that you're completely protected.

You can also ask the angels to watch over your loved ones (even when they're in a different location):

Lassie asked the angels and Archangel Michael (the protective angel) to watch over her son Quinn when he entered the military. When he was deployed to Afghanistan in 2003, Quinn and his team were headed up a steep embankment when he fell and injured his leg. Because of this injury, the team had to take another route. When they arrived at their post, they discovered that an ambush had been waiting for them atop the embankment where Quinn had fallen.

If they'd climbed to the top, they could have all been killed.

Two years later, Quinn fell 55 feet out of a helicopter without a parachute and landed on his back. Yet his only injury was a scraped elbow.

Lassie says, "Oh yes, I believe in angels, and I know they saved my son's life."

Not only do angels protect us from harm, they also bring us peace by making our lives a little easier, which includes helping us find lost items or whatever else we're looking for, as you'll read about in the next chapter.

Chapter Five

ANGELS HELP US FIND WHAT WE'RE LOOKING FOR

Nothing is ever lost in the eyes of God. Even though we may not know where an item is, God does. Acting as God's messengers, the angels can bring the item back into our possession, replace it with something better, or lead us to the location of the item.

Archangel Chamuel is the chief "finding angel," who helps us locate missing items. If you misplace your checkbook, keys, or sunglasses, call upon Chamuel and the angels for help. Sometimes the angels will guide you to the location of the item. Other times, the angels will bring the item to you and place it in a location where you'd previously looked for it, as Altaira experienced:

Altaira was cross-stitching one evening when her needle fell onto the floor.
She searched everywhere but couldn't
find it. Worried that her son or cat would
step on the needle, she asked her angels
to help her find it. She threaded another
needle and then left the room.

When she came back, the first needle
was sitting right next to her chair. She
says, "I know I looked there because I
even felt over the area of the carpet with
my hand." Even more remarkably, the
second needle that Altaira had threaded
was placed in a thread holder so that it
wouldn't fall out—something that Altaira
knows she didn't do.

Many people have told me that they've been
able to locate long-lost valuables after they called
upon the angels. I've heard countless stories of
people finding their wedding rings, heirlooms,
and other valuables. Sophia's story is especially
poignant:

Sophia treasured her moonstone and silver earrings, especially since she'd worn them during happy times with her son and other family members. So she grieved when she returned from the grocery store and discovered that one of the earrings she'd been wearing was missing.

She thoroughly checked her hair, clothing, purse, shopping bags, the kitchen, and her car. She worried that the earring had fallen off at the store or in the parking lot. Sophia said to her angels, "Please help the earring find its way back to me." She didn't know how it would happen, but something told her that her faith would be rewarded.

Two weeks later, after Sophia returned from the same grocery store, she walked through the garage to water the plants in her backyard. As she crossed by her car, a flash of silver caught her eye. It was her earring, slightly bent, but not in any way damaged. As she reached down to pick it up, tears of gratitude filled her eyes and she said, "Thank you, angels!" aloud. Sophia says, "I truly believe now, if I didn't before, that with a little bit of faith and lots of help from the angels, anything is possible!"

Not only can the angels locate missing objects, they can also negotiate their return in miraculous ways. After you ask the angels to return something to you, let go of the request and don't worry about how they'll answer your prayer. If you receive a feeling or a thought to go somewhere or do something, be sure to follow this guidance, as it may lead you directly to the object of your prayers, as Karen discovered:

After a long day at work, Karen was looking forward to going home. First, she needed to mail some bills and deposit checks at the bank. So on her way home, she stopped at the post office and headed toward the bank. But as she prepared to make her deposit, she realized that the checks were missing! Karen asked her angels, "Where could the checks be?" A soft voice replied, "Breathe in deeply, listen with your heart, and you will know." So Karen took in three deep breaths and listened.

She immediately heard, "You accidentally picked them up with the bills you mailed, and they're in the post office box." Karen's heart sank with the realization that the mail must have already been picked up by the mail carrier, and that her checks were already long gone.

The voice said to her, "Breathe in deeply and listen to your heart." Once Karen did so, her fears were calmed enough to hear the angels' next set of instructions: "Go to the post office. He was running late and he is there now collecting the mail. He will help you find the checks." So Karen raced to the post office, and sure enough, the mail carrier was pulling out the mail bins to place in his truck.

Karen explained the situation to him,

and the man kindly obliged by saying, "Oh, don't worry, we'll go through the mail together." Very soon they found the checks. As Karen thanked her angels, she heard them say, "Thank you, Karen, for listening. We did this together!"

In addition to finding lost objects, the angels can also guide you to the right job, a great home, wonderful friends, or anything else you need:

Joanie was driving by herself at night, en route from California to visit her mother in Texas. It was getting late, so Joanie decided to pull off the highway and find a hotel for the night. Out in the middle of nowhere, there only seemed to be seedy, unsafe motels along the route. So Joanie said aloud, "Okay, angels, please help me find a safe and comfortable place to stay tonight." She was guided to an exit where she found a newly constructed hotel. The hotel's lobby was lavishly decorated with angel statues, and they had a wonderful room available for Joanie.

The angels can help you with everything—from the seemingly trivial to matters of life and death. In the next three chapters, we'll look at ways to work with your angels to heal and improve your relationships, career, and health.

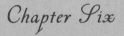

Chapter Six

ANGELIC HELP
WITH
RELATIONSHIPS

It's easy to be at peace when you're alone in meditation. Yet, real spiritual growth comes from learning how to navigate relationships peacefully. How do you stay centered and loving when people around you seem to pull you down? Once again, the angels offer very practical and effective help.

As a former psychotherapist, I've studied relationships for decades. Although many types of therapy geared toward this area are highly effective, I've found that the angels' work in this area far exceeds what humans can do when it comes to manifesting and healing relationships. So whether it's a romantic, familial, parent-child, or friendship relationship in question, you're very wise to work in partnership with the angels.

Your Love Life

The angels can help you with romance, whether you're in a committed relationship or single. If you're looking for your soul mate, the "romance angels" can help you find your special someone. A powerful method for invoking the angels' help is to find a quiet location where you won't be interrupted, and write a letter that starts like this:

Dear Guardian Angels of My Soul Mate,

Then, pour out your heart to these angels in the body of the letter. It doesn't matter whether you know who your soul mate is, because the angels do. Then conclude the letter by saying something like:

I know that my soul mate is looking for me with the same fervor as I am looking for him/her. Thank you for guiding us to meet, love, and experience a joyful and harmonious relationship based upon mutual respect, integrity, shared interests, and passionate romance. Thank you for clearly guiding me in ways that I can easily understand so that I may enjoy this relationship now.

Several couples have met at my workshops, and their relationships have blossomed as a result of the shared goal of working with the angels together. Usually at my workshops I ask audience members who are seeking a soul mate to raise their hands and then look around the room to see who else has their hands raised. Then I invoke a group of angels known as the "romance angels," Cupid-like cherubs who help us recover our playful delight in life. Between these angels and the hand-raising exercise, at least five couples who met at my workshops are now married as a result.

The romance angels can also infuse new passion into existing relationships. Ask them to help you and your partner recover your playful side, which is an important ingredient of romance. The angels say that many couples become overly focused on work and responsibilities, and they need to make time for playful and loving interactions. The romance angels can help you find time for this important endeavor, and also give you the energy to carry through.

Relationships with Friends

Our relationships sometimes change when we commit to a spiritual path, which includes working with the angels. If you have a friendship that began when you were focused on the material world, you may feel yourself pulling away from that friend as your focus becomes more spirit-centered. For one thing, your interests may grow apart. For another, the Law of Attraction says that we're attracted to people who are on the same wavelength as we are. So, someone who's focused on love and peace won't be attracted to someone whose focus is fear.

Ask your angels to help you through these shifts and changes in your relationships. Ask them to bring peaceful resolutions to any relationships that are ending. The angels can also bring you wonderful new friends, if you'll simply ask.

Relationships with Family Members

In the same way, your family interactions may change as you become more spiritually focused. If you come from a more traditional family, they may at first worry about your spirituality. Don't try to convince or convert anyone to your new way of thinking. The best way to handle this sort of situation is to be peaceful and happy. In that way, you're a walking advertisement for the benefits of living on the spiritual path. As people notice your peacefulness, they'll soon ask you about the secret to your happiness.

The angels guide us to release resentment and anger as an avenue to peace. Most of us have experienced pain in our relationships with family, friends, and lovers. The angels ensure that this pain doesn't ruin our present and future health and happiness.

If someone has performed an action that you feel is unforgivable, the angels won't ask you to change your mind and say, "What they did is okay." Instead, the angels want you to release the poisonous anger within your mind and body. When we hold resentment, we attract similar relationships and situations to us.

If you're tired of unhealthy relationship patterns, the likely culprit is unforgiveness toward a family member. The word *forgiveness* is a synonym for "releasing toxins," and replacing them with health and peace. The angels can help you with this, if you'll ask.

One effective way to release emotional toxins is to call upon Archangels Michael and Jeremiel as you're falling asleep. That's because when you're sleeping, you're more open to angelic intervention. When you're awake, your ego's fear can block the angels' help.

Say to the archangels, either silently or aloud:

*"I ask that you clear away any old anger,
pain, resentment, judgments, bitterness, or
unforgiveness from my mind, body, and emotions. I am willing to exchange pain for peace.
I now release to you anything that may be
blocking my awareness of peace, especially
within my relationships."*

When you awaken, you'll notice a positive
shift. It doesn't matter whether you recall your
dream interactions with the archangels or not,
as their work is on the unconscious level.

The angels can clear old issues with people
who are living or deceased. These healings don't
mean that you have to reignite a relationship
with the person. The intention is to clear the
path for you to feel love, peace, and harmony in
all areas of your life.

Children

Dozens of parents have told me that they
were successfully able to adopt a baby or con-

ceive after they asked for the angels' help, such as in Mary's example:

Mary and her husband were frustrated by the process of applying for and waiting for a baby to adopt. Still, they didn't give up hope. One morning as Mary was leaving work, she noticed an angel pin in its original packaging on the ground near her car door. She wondered why an angel pin would be at the construction company where she worked, since she was the only female employee.

She pinned the angel on her purse and hoped that it was a positive sign. That evening, Mary asked her angels for help with the adoption. The next morning, the adoption agency called with the good news that they had a baby for Mary and her husband. They brought home their son, John, the following day, and he just celebrated his fifth birthday.

After a baby is brought home, the angels continue to offer support. The two archangels who specialize in children-related issues are Gabriel and Metatron. Gabriel tends to the early part of childhood, from pregnancy through the toddler stage. As the child matures, Metatron takes over as a firm but loving custodian. His chief role is to develop and protect the child's spiritual nature.

Parents can call on Gabriel and Metatron for extra support with childhood behavioral issues. For health or dietary concerns, Raphael is the archangel to call upon. For any serious behavioral difficulties such as drug use or aggressive tendencies, ask Archangel Michael for help. Many of these difficulties occur when highly sensitive youths unwittingly absorb negative energy from their surroundings. Ask Michael to "vacuum" your child, which is a term the angels use to describe their process of clearing someone of these lower energies. I've seen complete behavioral turnarounds occur as a result of Michael vacuuming a person—with results exceeding the psychotherapy methods I studied in my university and hospital training.

Perhaps it's the angels' pure love, or maybe it's the fact that they're completely unrestricted by fear or Earthly concerns. Whatever it is that effects miracles, I've seen and heard of many of them concerning children helped by angels. This story, which I first wrote about in my book *The Care and Feeding of Indigo Children*, is an example:

A woman named Josie approached me at my workshop with tears in her eyes and her arms outstretched, waiting to embrace me. She exclaimed that after reading my books about working with angels, she'd experienced Divine intervention with her 13-year-old son, Chris.

"Chris was out of control before I began working with his angels," Josie explained to me. "He wouldn't come home on time, and he was using drugs. His schoolwork was a mess. Then my aunt brought home one of your books, and I read how to talk to Chris's angels. I really didn't believe in angels at the time.

I thought they were like Santa Claus: a myth. But I was desperate to help my son, so I gave it a try.

"I silently talked to Chris's guardian angels, even though I wasn't really sure I was doing it right. I wasn't even sure that he had angels, the way he was acting like a devil and all! But I saw results almost immediately. I kept talking to those angels every night."

I asked Josie how Chris was doing these days.

"He's great!" she beamed. "He's happy, off drugs, and he's doing well in school."

Relationship Healing with the Angels

You can heal misunderstandings by talking to the other person's guardian angels. Although the angels can't violate anyone's free will, they will intervene into any situation that's affecting your peace—including relationship woes.

In these situations, close your eyes and center

yourself through breath. Then, hold the intention of talking with the other person's guardian angels. You can't make a mistake and do this incorrectly, as the intention is more important than the method you use.

Then, pour out your heart (either silently, in a letter, or aloud) to that person's angels. Tell them about your fears, anger, disappointments, and desires. Next, ask the angels to bring about peace in the relationship. Don't tell the angels how to do so, or you'll slow or miss the answer to your prayer. Allow the infinite creative wisdom of God's Divine Mind to come up with an ingenious solution that will delight everyone involved in the situation.

Have you ever wished that you could go back in time and take back something you said, or handle a situation differently? Well, the angels can help you with this desire through a process called "undoing." Think of the actions or words that you'd like to rewrite, and say to the angels:

"I ask that all effects of this mistake

be undone in all directions of time,
for everyone involved."

This method often results in those involved forgetting about what happened, as if it had never occurred. It puts a new meaning to the phrase "Forgive and forget."

The angels say that when another person annoys or angers us, it's because we're seeing something in them that we don't like about ourselves. In other words, we're projecting our ego issues that we aren't aware of, or don't want to admit to. Everyone has ego issues, so they're nothing to feel ashamed of. In fact, projection is a wonderful tool that helps us become aware of our own ego issues so that we can work on them.

The angels recommend that if we become annoyed or angered at someone, we can say:

"I am willing to release that part of me that
irritates me when I think of you."

This doesn't mean that your own actions

resemble the actions of the person who annoyed you. It simply means that some shadow within you recognizes the shadow within the other person.

When we admit honestly to this projection process using the angel's affirmation above, we're able to shift to a higher perspective. We can then see ourselves and other people through the eyes of the angels.

The angels overlook people's surface personalities and ego issues. They instead focus upon the light and love that's within every person, regardless of outward appearances. The more we see the goodness within others, the more we can see it within ourselves.

The angels say that every relationship serves an ultimate purpose, even short-lived ones. When the purpose of the relationship has been served, the attraction between the two people diminishes. This is one reason why relationships sometimes end.

The angels can help us with relationship endings, including making difficult decisions about leaving, giving us the courage and strength we need to endure a breakup, providing for everyone involved, and helping us heal.

When Annette's husband left her and her two small sons, she was devastated emotionally and financially. Almost symbolic of how helpless she felt, her toddler's stroller was locked in her dilapidated car's trunk and no one could open it, so she had to carry her toddler in her arms wherever they went. After six months of struggling, she finally decided to ask the angels for help. In particular, Annette called upon Archangel Michael, whom she'd worked with previously.

Annette was guided to release her hurt and anger toward her ex-husband by writing him a heartfelt letter and then burning it. After the letter was in ashes, Annette began seeing bright blue flashes of light that told her that Archangel Michael was with her.

The next day, Annette was guided to remove all of her ex-husband's belongings from her car. She asked the angels to remove any negativity from herself, her children, her home, and her car. As Annette was cleaning the last of her ex-husband's papers from the car, the trunk of the car popped open on its own. Annette couldn't believe it! She gratefully removed the stroller from the trunk, thanking the angels profusely for helping her.

She went in the house and the telephone rang. It was her nephew, who rarely called, saying that he'd told his neighbor about her situation. The neighbor was selling a beautiful white car in perfect condition for $5,000, but he was willing to let Annette have it for $2,000. Annette cried when the car was delivered, as it was beyond anything she'd hoped for.

She says, "I knew when I saw the white car roll into my driveway that it was a gift from the angels. I am overwhelmed by how much 'luck' I've had since I asked the angels to help my life. They still look after me on a daily basis, letting me know that they're with me through their flashing blue, violet, and green lights. I never want for anything, as all of my day-to-day needs are met, thanks to the angels."

The angels can help us with every relation-ship issue, whether it's with a spouse, family member, friend, or even a stranger. The angels also guide and protect our relationships at work. After all, we spend a lot of time with co-workers, employers, clients, and other people we come into contact with at our workplace. In the next chapter, we'll explore how the angels want to help us with our career and life purpose.

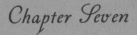
ANGELIC HELP
FOR YOUR
CAREER
AND
LIFE PURPOSE

One of the main questions I'm asked by audience members is: "Can the angels tell me about my life purpose?" The underlying question in this query is usually: "What career would be most meaningful for me?"

Since we usually spend eight or more hours of each day working, it makes sense to want meaningful employment. This is something more than a job that pays the bills. It's a career that you feel passionate about, and that you believe is making a positive difference in the world. And if it pays a good salary, well, that's even better.

We each have an important and much-needed life purpose involving our natural talents, passions, and interests. Our life purpose helps other people, animals, or the environment in some way. The angels ask us to focus on providing some type of service, and not to worry about the money or accolades we'll receive. They say, "Serve a purpose, and your purpose will then serve you in return." The angels can bring you whatever support you need in this area.

The Archangels and Careers

The archangels are happy to help you with all aspects of your career. Here are some of the roles that specific archangels can fulfill:

Ariel: This archangel helps those interested in environmental, nature, or animal-related careers. Ariel also helps in the manifestation of money or other supplies needed for your life purpose and day-to-day expenses.

Azrael: If your career involves grief counseling or guiding people through losses (such as working at a hospital, hospice, counseling center, and the like), this archangel can guide your words and actions to comfort and empower the bereaved.

Chamuel: The "finding archangel" will help you locate the career or job you're seeking. Chamuel will also help you retain your peacefulness, helping you find the best job.

Gabriel: The messenger archangel helps teachers, journalists, writers, and those who want to work with children. If you feel guided to write, Gabriel will motivate and guide you. If you'd like to help children in some way, ask Gabriel for a Divine assignment.

Haniel: The archangel of grace is wonderful to invoke when going out on a job interview, attending meetings, or any-time you want to be extra-articulate and graceful.

Jophiel: The archangel of beauty helps to keep the energy clean and high at your workplace, and to keep your thoughts about your career positive. She also helps artists, creative types, anyone involved in the beauty business, and feng shui practitioners with all aspects of their careers.

Metatron: If your career involves ado-lescents or energetic children, Metatron can help you. He can give you a Divine assignment if you'd like to work with adolescents; and Metatron is also a won-derful motivator and organizer, so call upon him if you need assistance with your get-up-and-go.

Michael: Archangel Michael can help you discern your life's purpose and the next step to take in your career. One of the best ways to start the process is to write him a letter, inquiring about your best career or educational choices. Michael is one of the loudest archangels, so you probably won't have any trouble hearing him. Write his replies below your questions in your letter, so you have a record of his career guidance.

Michael's speaking style is very much to the point. He's quite loving, but he's also very blunt. For this reason, Michael is a wonderful archangel to call upon for the courage to change or improve your career. He'll help you change to a better job; start your own business; and speak your truth lovingly to co-workers, bosses, and clients.

Michael is also amazing at fixing electronic and mechanical items such as computers, cars, fax machines, and such.

Raguel: If your work involves relationships with clients, co-workers, and mediation (such as marriage counseling), Archangel Raguel can ensure harmonious interactions.

Raphael: If you're in a healing career, or feel guided to be a healer, Raphael can help you. As the chief healing angel, Raphael assists with all aspects of healing careers. Raphael can guide and help you to select the healing modality that you'd most enjoy, manifest tuition for your healing education, open and run a healing center, find the best employment in a healing field or establish a successful private practice, and guide you with the best actions and words during your healing sessions.

Sandalphon: This archangel helps with careers in the arts, especially music. Call upon Sandalphon as a muse to inspire you, as a teacher to guide your creative process, and as an agent to market your creative projects.

Uriel: The archangel of light can illuminate your mind with wise ideas and concepts. Call upon Uriel for problem solving, brainstorming, or important conversations.

Zadkiel: This archangel helps you improve your memory, and he's a wonderful helpmate for students or anyone who needs to remember names, figures, or other important information.

The Angels at Work

The angels will work overtime to help you with your career. Just ask, and they will screen your phone calls and keep away unnecessary time-wasters.

Angels can also guide suitable customers to your business. A wonderful prayer to say in the morning is:

"I ask that everyone who would receive blessings from my product (or services) be given the time, money, and whatever else they need to purchase my product (or services) today."

I've spoken with several successful shop owners who use a similar prayer with great success. In visiting these stores, I'm thrilled to see that they're filled with happy, paying customers.

Ask the angels to help you have fun at work, and they'll inject each day with joyful, meaningful moments. If you need something, such as a new computer, new inventory, or a bigger office, ask the angels for help in this regard. If you need ideas, connections, or energy, again the angels can come to your aid.

The angels can help you with every big and small detail connected to your work life because they love you and care about you. They want you to be at peace, and they also know that you're happiest when you feel good about the way you spend your day.

The angels want to help us feel good all the time, and that includes healing our loved ones if a health challenge arises. In the next chapter, we'll discuss some of the ways in which angels watch over our health, ensuring continued peace of mind, body, and spirit.

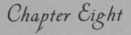

Chapter Eight

HEALING
WITH THE
ANGELS

Nothing is impossible for God and the angels. They can heal any condition, increase our motivation to exercise, and eliminate or reduce cravings for unhealthful foods or substances. All that's required on our part is a crystal clear decision that we want to heal, and a willingness to surrender the situation entirely to God and the angels.

The angels work in conjunction with Jesus, Buddha, or other deities, so you needn't worry that angelic healing interferes with your religious beliefs or constraints.

You can ask God to send healing angels to another person. As stated earlier, the angels won't violate someone else's free will by imposing an unwanted healing upon them (remember that not everyone wants to heal for various personal reasons known only to themselves). However, the *presence* of the angels has a calming effect that is always helpful and healthy, so it's a good idea to invoke angels for those dealing with health challenges.

Archangel Raphael is the primary angel who conducts and oversees healings. He's assisted by "healing angels" who work in precise concert with him to orchestrate miraculous healings. Raphael's halo is emerald green, which is the energetic color of pure love. Raphael surrounds injured or diseased areas with emerald green light.

Sometimes the angels heal by guiding us to wonderful human health practitioners. After you ask for the angels' help, pay close attention to repetitive ideas or feelings that ask you to contact certain doctors or health facilities. Remember that you can always ask the angels to speak louder, or to explain anything that you don't understand.

Holly's story illustrates how the angels can miraculously heal us, provided that we ask for their help and then get out of the way so that they can do their work:

Holly survived a head-on automobile collision, but with her right ankle completely shattered by the impact, she felt as though an important part of her life had died. An avid hiker, jogger, and dancer, Holly was now barely able to stand and walk. She couldn't wear the pointy high-heeled shoes she'd always loved, and she wasn't able to dance around the kitchen as she'd regularly done while fixing her family's dinner.

Without the use of her right ankle, life seemed colorless, and Holly became depressed. She was limping, in pain, and her doctor was recommending surgery to permanently fuse her ankle with a screw to completely restrict the movement of her right foot.

Holly had read many books about angels, and she fervently believed in God, yet she'd always been the one in control of her life, never asking others for help . . . not even God. A self-professed "control freak," Holly always believed that if she didn't take care of things herself, they wouldn't get done. However, now she was depressed and ready to ask for help.

After reading the healings described in my book *Angel Medicine,* Holly had an epiphany and realized that she deserved the same help that others had received from God and the angels. She said to herself, *I am worthy of a miracle!* She also realized that her previous method of trying to control everything and use "mind over matter" wasn't working.

She recalls, "For the first time in my life, I let go. I realized I didn't have to handle this alone. I let go of the fear, the hurt, and the depression. The only thing I asked for was that my healing occur while I was sleeping, as I knew I'd ask too many questions if it happened while I was awake!"

After Holly asked God and the angels for a healing, she curled up with her three dogs and fell asleep. Normally during the night, Holly's dogs would stir and ask to be let outside, but this evening was completely different and they slept until daybreak.

Holly, on the other hand, was abruptly awoken by electrical impulses that made her body twitch. She felt both hot and cold as the electrical impulses moved through her body. The room was filled with the same feeling of static electricity.

Holly felt lighter than she ever had before, and she knew in that moment that she'd been healed. A voice said to Holly, "Stand up," so she swung her legs over the edge of the bed. The dogs still slept.

Holly says, "The foot that was for the most part immobilized had regained full range of motion! My right foot matched every angle and rotation of the left. I stood up, and for the first time in a year and a half, I was pain free. I could place all my weight on that foot and walk without a limp."

Holly now dances, jogs, and wears

high-heeled shoes again. She remarks, "I'm doing what science says is impossible. I simply had to believe. I simply had to ask for it. Thank You, dearest God, for sending Your archangels to me. I finally have my life back."

In addition to healing human bodies, the angels can also heal animals. Again, it's just a matter of asking:

Andrea's cat, Jesus, was very ill. He wouldn't move or eat, so she took him to the vet, where he was diagnosed with an infection and kidney stones. A few days later, he was still in the animal hospital with a high fever. Around 4:30 P.M., when Andrea called to check on her cat, the vet warned that her cat might not live.

Crying, Andrea hung up the phone and implored the angels to heal her cat. After 30 minutes of talking with her angels, Andrea felt peaceful. She heard a voice say, "Your kitty will get well and be as if nothing happened."

The next morning when she called the animal hospital, a nurse told Andrea that her cat's temperature returned to normal about 5:30 the evening before. This was the same time when Andrea felt peaceful after talking with her angels! Today, you'd never know that Andrea's cat had ever been ill, just as the angels promised.

Healthy Lifestyles

While the angels are happy to help us with health crises, they're also very involved with preventive medicine so that we stay healthy and vital throughout our lives. You've most likely felt or heard your angels nudge you to change your diet, exercise more, or do something else to improve your health.

Many people find that soon after they begin working with angels, their taste for certain foods and beverages changes. Some people even lose the ability to comfortably digest their former dietary favorites.

This is part of the upward energy vibration shift that occurs when you're surrounded by angels. In the same way that the Law of Attraction means that you're attracted to people who hold similar feelings and beliefs to your own, so will you find your attractions to foods and beverages changing.

Some people naturally and easily improve their diet, yet many of us need angelic help. I had terrible headaches soon after I began writing angel books. Since I'd never had them before in my entire life, I knew that something was wrong. I asked Archangel Raphael about this, and I immediately heard (through my feelings and thoughts) that my daily chocolate eating was the culprit. He explained that chocolate was lowering my energy, which caused a clash whenever I connected with the angels. It was kind of like low-pressure and high-pressure weather systems colliding and causing a storm.

I was horrified by this news, as I craved chocolate almost constantly. I wondered how I could go even one day without it, so I asked Raphael to help me. That was in 1996, and I haven't craved or wanted chocolate since that evening. He completely healed me of all desires for it, which was no minor miracle for a former chocoholic like me. The headaches also vanished and haven't returned.

The angels aren't prudes or morality police, but they do know that some of us need to live chemical-free lives for optimal health and happiness, so they often guide us to detoxify and steer clear of alcohol, sugar, caffeine, nicotine, and other drugs. The angels have helped me and many others to be free of chemicals and cravings.

In addition to diet issues, the angels also steer us toward healthy exercise programs that match our interests and energy levels. They often guide us to yoga, because it helps us focus and meditate; as well as strengthen our muscles, clear our chakras, and have more energy.

The angels also love us to spend time in nature, as the magical energy of fresh air, trees, flowers, plants, water, and sunshine refreshes and renews us.

In addition, the angels urge us to get plenty of rest. This guidance also includes ensuring that bedrooms are quiet, beds are comfortable, and that bedding and pillows are allergen free.

If you've had feelings or thoughts urging you to engage in any of these healthy lifestyle changes, that's a sign that you're hearing your angels' guidance. If you need help with motivation, energy, time, money, or anything else in support of making these changes, just ask.

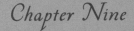

Chapter Nine

ANGELS ON EARTH

*Y*ou may have met an angel in human form who gave you a comforting message or performed a heroic deed. Angels can appear in human bodies when it's necessary to save a life or to help someone really hear what they have to say.

Incarnated angels look like ordinary people. Sometimes they're well dressed, and sometimes they're dressed in rags. These angels usually take physical form temporarily, just long enough to perform a Heavenly function. However, some angels live entire lifetimes as humans, when a family, hospital, school, or other group requires long-term angelic help.

Here's an example of how some angels in human form helped Susan:

One cold winter, Susan's* furnace went out. She called appliance companies but discovered that she couldn't afford the cost of a replacement furnace, nor repairs. The next day, an unmarked white van pulled up in front of her home. Two men in unmarked uniforms informed Susan that they were sent to deliver and install her new furnace.

When Susan protested that she hadn't ordered a new furnace, the men said that they'd install it and she could later discuss the finances with their office. Susan never heard from the men again, and she didn't know what company to call to inquire about paying for the furnace. She just knew that her angels had arranged for heat for herself and her family.

Angels help us in miraculous ways. Instead of praying for the money to replace her furnace,

Susan simply asked for heat to be restored to her home. If she'd insisted that God give her money because she believed that was her only route to having a furnace, the answer to her prayer may not have readily come.

In the same way, Tracy discovered that the angels are unceasingly generous with time and money:

> Tracy and her baby daughter were at the airport checking in for their flight home; however the airline said that Tracy's ticket was invalid and that she'd have to buy another one to be allowed on the flight. She didn't have the money for a second ticket, so she sat down and began crying.
>
> A gentle hand touched Tracy's shoulder. It was a well-dressed elderly woman who asked if she could help. When Tracy explained her predicament, the woman immediately bought her a replacement ticket. Tracy thanked the woman profusely, and then a moment later the woman vanished.

When Tracy boarded the airplane, she was happy to find that this same woman was seated next to her, and she comforted Tracy and her baby during the flight. When they landed, Tracy again thanked her benefactress for the ticket and comforting words. Yet, immediately after they disembarked, the woman again vanished. Tracy has no doubt that the woman was an angel in disguise.

An angel may come into our lives in human form for a brief relationship, to provide us with protection, to steer us through a major life intersection, or to give us support and guidance. These beings may exit our lives as quickly as they entered, because they've fulfilled their angelic function:

Anna had been styling Betty's hair every Friday morning at 9 A.M. for three months. One Thursday evening, Betty called Anna to change the next morning's appointment to 8 A.M. As a result, Anna arrived at her shop an hour earlier than normal. Ten minutes later, a 6.0-magnitude earthquake shook her shop (it was the Whittier Narrows earthquake of October 1987).

During the quake, Anna's mobile home fell over and a utility pole crashed into her awnings. If not for Betty's earlier appointment, which got her out of the house, Anna would have likely suffered injuries or worse. Betty never arrived for her appointment, and Anna never heard from her again. After all, Betty had served her Heavenly function of protecting Anna's life.

Sometimes Heaven asks us to fulfill the function of an angel. Have you ever counseled a friend or client and said something so wise and comforting that you wondered where those words came from? That's an example of God speaking through you as a messenger angel.

Other times, it's very clear when you're being tapped on the shoulder to act as an Earth angel, which is what happened to Kathy:

A licensed nurse, Kathy thought about stopping to help when she saw a terrible auto wreck on the other side of the interstate. But she worried about getting across the fast-moving traffic. Something inside of her told her to stop anyway. As she got out of her car, a woman approached and called Kathy by her first name, although they'd never met before. The woman said that the people in the accident needed her assistance. When Kathy replied, "I can't get across the road," the woman said, "I will help you."

The woman stepped out in the middle of the busy interstate and put her hands up to stop the big semitrailers. She grabbed Kathy's arm and led her across to a young man lying in the road who desperately needed medical attention. Kathy looked over her shoulder to thank the woman, but she'd disappeared.

Kathy administered CPR to, and prayed with, the young man until the ambulance arrived. She later inquired about the woman, but no one else had seen her. Kathy is sure that she was a guardian angel, and that she herself was used in the service of an angel that night.

Most people who meet an angel in human form don't initially realize that the helpful person is an angel. It's only afterward when the angel vanishes from sight that its true identity becomes known:

One extremely foggy night, Barbara and her friend Lorraine worried about driving home from school safely after a day of teaching. The fog was so thick that they had difficulty finding their car in the school parking lot. Just as Barbara was reluctantly getting behind the wheel to drive, a well-dressed man appeared from out of nowhere.

"Move over," he said authoritatively. Neither woman felt afraid, and somehow trusted the man and his judgment. On the drive home, they both felt sleepy, as if in a dreamlike stupor.

Barbara recalls, "I came back to reality just as we pulled into the driveway to find that my husband and Lorraine's husband were waiting for us, relieved that we'd made it home safely." Lorraine dashed into the house, while Barbara pondered what had happened. The man had disappeared, and Barbara was seated behind the steering wheel without any recollection of how she'd gotten there. To this day, Lorraine and Barbara are both puzzled, but they believe that an angel came to their rescue that night.

Angels take on human form to provide physical assistance, like the angel-man who drove Barbara and Lorraine safely home through the fog. They also briefly incarnate during times of stress and crisis, when we can't hear the still, small voice of Spirit. In those cases, angels take human form so that we'll pay attention to their important messages and warnings, as in Patricia's case:

Patricia was driving through an intersection when she heard a huge crash. As she opened her eyes, she realized she'd been in an accident. Patricia slowly sat up and noticed a woman standing at her car window. "Turn off the car!" the woman said. "It's off," Patricia replied, not realizing that the engine was still running. The woman repeated, "Turn the key to turn it off." Patricia complied, and the woman disappeared.

Firefighters and paramedics used the Jaws of Life to pull Patricia from her car. One of the men remarked, "Good thing you turned off your car. It was leaking gas all over the road, and one spark from the ignition would have blown you sky-high." When Patricia explained that the woman had instructed her to turn off the car, the man said, "What woman? No one was at your car before us. They couldn't have gotten to you until the car was towed out of traffic, off to the side of the road." That's when Patricia realized she'd been saved by an angel.

Whether they're incarnated in human form or in the spirit world, the angels are here to implement God's plan of peace, one person at a time. That means the angels want to help you with whatever will bring *you* peace. If you don't know what that is, you can ask the angels for guidance on setting healthy intentions for yourself. The angels can also give you the time, motivation, energy, and whatever else you need to act on your Divine guidance.

The angels love you more than words can convey. They love you unconditionally, and they appreciate and value your gifts, talents, and Divine mission. More than anything, your angels wish you to enjoy utter peace and happiness. They're available around-the-clock to help you with this endeavor. All you need to do is ask.

Chapter Ten

FREQUENTLY ASKED QUESTIONS ABOUT ANGELS

Here are some of the questions that are frequently posed by audience members at my lectures, and by readers of my books. While I don't claim to know all the answers, I'm a good listener, and these responses are the ones I received by asking God and the angels. I encourage you to ask them your questions and listen to the replies you get as well.

Q: Why can't I hear my angels?

A: The two main reasons why people can't seem to hear their angels is that they're trying too hard to make something happen, and they're unaware of or unsure about the angelic messages they're receiving.

It's important that you don't strain, or try too hard, to hear them. Easy does it. Remember that the angels are more motivated than you are to have a conversation. Let them do the work, while you stay in a receptive state instead of chasing after their voice.

Quiet your mind through breath, then close your eyes and ask your angels to help you feel peaceful. Then, ask your angels a question. Notice the impressions that come to you in the form of ideas, physical or emotional feelings, visions, or words. It's impossible to get nothing, since angels always reply to every prayer and question, and because you're always thinking and feeling—two channels of angelic communication.

Honor the thoughts and feelings that come to you, especially if they're repetitive, loving, and inspiring. Often the angels' messages are very simple and seemingly unrelated to your question or prayer. If you're still unsure about the validity or meaning of the message, ask the angels to give you a clear sign or additional information.

Sometimes people can't hear their angels because of lifestyle habits. Possible interference to clear Divine communication can include a noisy environment and chemicals or animal products in the diet. If you've been getting strong feelings or ideas to clean up your lifestyle, ask the angels for motivation and help in doing so.

Q: I've asked my angels for help, but nothing seems to happen.

A: The most frequent reason why prayers seem to go unanswered is because Divine guidance (the angels' response to your prayers in the form of instructions and advice that will lead you to your desires) hasn't been noticed or is being ignored. If you expect one specific type of answer to a prayer, you may not notice something that differs from your expectations. For instance, when I prayed to meet and marry my soul mate, I received Divine guidance to go to a yoga class, which is where I ultimately met my husband. If I hadn't listened to the Divine guidance to attend this class, I may have assumed that my prayers were going unanswered.

Some people don't trust the Divine guidance they receive. For instance, if you pray for an improved financial situation, you may get strong impressions to open a business or change jobs. Yet, if you feel intimidated by the idea of changing jobs or running a company, you may ignore this guidance and assume that the angels aren't helping you financially.

A third reason falls under the category of "Divine timing." Some prayers are instantly answered, while others need time to "cook" before all the factors fall into place. Prayers may not be answered until we feel ready or deserving of receiving their fulfillment.

Q: Do you worship angels?

A: No. The angels don't want us to worship them. They want all glory to go to God.

Q: Why don't the angels save everyone, especially innocent children?

A: This question speaks to one of life's deep mysteries, and the answer may be unknowable. Some people choose not to fight for their lives during illness or injuries, and other people don't listen to their Divine guidance that might spare them. It seems that we all have a "time" to return home to Heaven, which our souls predetermine prior to our incarnation. While we wish that everyone would choose healthy and long lives on Earth, apparently that's not part of every soul's path or desires.

Q: What if what I'm asking for isn't God's will for me?

A: Some fear that God is *willing* their suffering, and they're afraid of violating a greater will than their own. Yet, if we truly believe that God is loving, and if we trust that God is good, then why would the Creator will anything but love and goodness for us? One who is all love would never "test" us, or use pain as a way to make us grow. Wouldn't we be more useful to God's plan if our energy and health were vibrant and radiant?

God is omnipresent, within each of us. This means that God's will is everywhere, overlapping your own. And a loving God would never want you to suffer in any way, just as you'd never will your own children to suffer. It's true that you can grow through pain, but it's also true that you can grow through peace.

God usually has higher standards for us than we do for ourselves. Very often, we ask for too little, while God stands by, unable to offer more lest our free will be violated. Ask for whatever will bring you peace, and Heaven will happily help you.

Q: I was raised to believe that I should only talk to God or Jesus. Is it blasphemous to talk to angels?

A: This fear stems from some organized religions' interpretation of spiritual texts. If you truly believe that you should only speak with God, Jesus, or some other spiritual being, then don't violate that belief. To do so would cause unnecessary fear, and we certainly don't want to add to that negative emotion.

However, do consider this: The word *angel*, as stated earlier, means "messenger of God." Angels are gifts from the Creator who act like Heavenly postal carriers, bringing messages to and from the Creator and the Created. They operate with Divine precision in delivering trustworthy guidance to us. And just like any gift, the giver (the Creator) wishes us to enjoy and use the gift. The Bible and other spiritual texts are filled with positive accounts of people talking to angels, and this natural phenomenon carries into the present day.

Q: How do I know that I'm really speaking to an angel and not just making it up?

A: True Divine guidance is uplifting, inspiring, motivational, positive, and loving. Angel messages always discuss how to improve something: an outlook, one's health, relationships, the environment, the world, and so on. Angels generally repeat the message through your feelings, thoughts, visions, and hearing until you take the advised action. If you're unsure if a message is real or not, wait awhile, as true Divine guidance repeats itself, while false guidance eventually fades away if ignored.

Watch out for the very common "impostor phenomenon," in which the ego tries to convince you that you're not qualified to talk to angels and that you don't have intuitive or psychic abilities. Know that this message is fear and ego based.

God and the angels all speak in loving and positive words. If you ever hear negative words from anyone, living or not, stop talking to them and immediately pray for the assistance of Archangel Michael. He'll escort lower energies away and protect you from negativity.

Talking with angels is a pleasant, joyful experience. Whether you hear them, see them, feel their presence, or receive new insights, you'll certainly enjoy connecting with them.

Q: If I work with angels, am I shirking my responsibility for taking control of my own life and my own personal growth?

A: Some people feel that they're "cheating" by requesting Divine intervention. They believe that we're supposed to suffer in order to learn and grow, and that we're responsible for getting ourselves in and out of jams. Yet the angels say that while we can grow through suffering, we can grow even faster through peace. And our peacefulness inspires others in ways that suffering cannot.

The angels won't do everything for you, though. They're more like teammates who ask you to pass the ball as you collectively move toward each goal. As you ask them for help, the angels will sometimes create a miraculous intervention. But more often, they'll help you by delivering Divine guidance so that you can help yourself.

≈ ≈

ABOUT
THE
AUTHOR

*D*oreen **Virtue** holds B.A., M.A., and Ph.D. degrees in counseling psychology, and is a life-long clairvoyant who works with the angelic realm. She is the author of *Assertiveness for Earth Angels, How to Hear Your Angels,* and *The Angel Therapy® Handbook,* among other works. Her products are available in most languages worldwide.

Doreen has appeared on *Oprah,* CNN, *The View,* and other television and radio programs, and she writes regular columns for *Woman's World* and *Spirit & Destiny* magazines. For more information on Doreen and the workshops she presents, please visit: www.AngelTherapy.com.

You can listen to Doreen's live weekly radio show, and call her for a reading, by visiting HayHouseRadio.com®.

ANGEL THERAPY®

HAY HOUSE TITLES
OF RELATED INTEREST